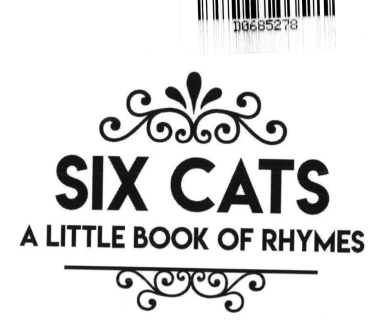

SIX CATS
A LITTLE BOOK OF RHYMES

Kathleen Braden

With an Introduction by Henri, le Chat Noir

Photographs by Kathleen Braden

Cover design by Anna Stiles

Publisher: Kathleen Braden

ISBN: 9798583084647

Dedicated to fans of Henri and people everywhere who love cats

INTRODUCTION BY HENRI, LE CHAT NOIR

I am of two minds about this collection of rhymes. On the one paw, I think any piece of art devoted to cats is a laudable endeavor. What better or more fascinating topic could one take on? However, given that myself and my compatriots are the subject of this work, I am somewhat concerned that these particular cats may not rise to the occasion once brought into the light. Many days they do not rise at all.

It is particularly commendable that the author, my caretaker, has taken great pains to address the common misconception that humans can "own" cats. Besides the obvious insult to our autonomy, this would somehow imply that cats "need" people. In truth, it is people that need us! How could humanity ever hope to rise above its flawed nature without a more noble example to aspire to? To be honest, I'm sometimes unsure just what humans bring to the table, other than food we are not allowed to jump up and eat.

Perhaps it is fitting that the author has chosen to complete this work without the inclusion of her progeny, the thieving filmmaker. He seemed less interested in examining the feline condition than exploiting it. I have long suspected he was behind my ignominious nickname, "Monsieur le Fluffy Butt". In this collection of short rhymes, at least there is an attempt to understand what it truly means to be a cat in an unfortunately human world. As much disdain as I have for humanity as a whole, my caretaker is quite catlike in her outlook on life. That is admirable.

That said, if we figure out how to work the can opener, we're out of here.

PROLOGUE

I present here some tales of six cats in one space:
two who moved in and took over the place;
one, a homebody; and two of some fame;
and one who has passed but I love her the same.

For loving a cat is easy to do
though they don't love us back- I don't think so, do
you?
They exploit and use us and shed everywhere,
pee in the bathtub, and scratch up the chair.

But a cat's a cat, as we know, for all that.

There are thin ones and fat ones
with fluff to admire,
and cats in their fur-abouts watching the fire,
and little cat feet that bring in the fog,
and it's said every time, they will outsmart a dog.

Cats on your bed, cats out in the barn,
city cats homeless, cats on the farm.
Cats living on ships far away from the shore,
cats in cafés or hosting a store.

Movie star cats- Thomasina and Sassy,
Oliver, Kedi, and Mustard with Lassie.
A witch's familiar – Pyewacket's the name,
Maru, Lil Bub of internet fame.
Keyboard Cat, Grumpy Cat, Kit gootchy-goo,
Felix, Sylvester, and Simon's Cat too.

The ominous lap cat of Don Corleone,
and old Bigglesworth, Dr. Evil's odd crony.
A no-name slob left out in the rain.
And Choupette Lagerfeld-rich, spoiled, and vain.

Hogwarts' Mrs. Norris and the Jellicle brood,
Grizabella, Pettipaws, and Rum Tum so rude.
For the cosmos, we have Jonesy and Jake
and Félicette, who was launched into space.

There's mayor cats with a policy plan:
Talkeetna's cat, Stubbs, and Halifax Stan.
White House cats Socks, Tabby, and Dixie,
Slippers, Tom Quartz, Blacky, and Misty.
And Downing Street's Larry caused a protocol matter
delaying Trump's limo (well, he *is* a good ratter).

It's just so easy to love any cat,
'cause a cat's still a cat, good or bad, for all that.

So put on your finest Cheshire Cat grin,
rejoice in our felines, and come enter in.
If you're a cat person, these rhymes are for you.
Cats rule the world; now, admit this is true.
For alone in an alley or pampered in wealth,
each cat is a Kingdom unto himself.

Prologue cat references: homage to Dylan Thomas, *A Child's Christmas in Wales*; *Fog* by Carl Sandburg; *The Three Lives of Thomasina* (1963); Sassy from *Homeward Bound: The Incredible Journey* (1993); *Oliver & Company* (1988); *Kedi* (2016 documentary); Mustard in Lassie television episode "The Cat That Came to Dinner" (1959); Pyewacket from *Bell, Book, and Candle* (1958); Don Corleone cat from *The Godfather* (1972); Bigglesworth from *Austin Powers*; No-name slob from *Breakfast at Tiffany's* (1961) and this author cries at the ending every time; Choupette Lagerfeld real-life heiress to Karl Lagerfeld fortune; Mrs. Norris from *Harry Potter*; Jellicle cats from T.S. Eliot poem and Andrew Lloyd Webber musical; Jonesy from film *Alien* (1979); Jake from film *The Cat from Outer Space* (1978); Felicette was first cat launched into space, Oct. 18, 1963, by France's Comité des Recherches Spatiales (she survived); Stubbs and Stan were real cats in respective cities; White House Cats: Socks – Bill Clinton, Tabby and Dixie – Abraham Lincoln, Slippers and Tom Quartz- Teddy Roosevelt, Blacky-Calvin Coolidge, Misty's full name was Misty Malarky Ying Yang and belonged to Amy Carter; Larry has lived at 10 Downing Street since 2011 and June, 2019 disrupted President Donald Trump's armored Cadillac by resting under the tires, causing a delay in the schedule; The Cheshire Cat, of course, from *Alice in Wonderland*.

LA CHANSON D'HENRI

I
In the city of Seattle
where rain comes down all day
at the animal shelter
along Interbay,
we'd met a cat we planned to adopt
and had almost signed all the docs.
She was simple and sweet, but nothing much more,
when with a strong wind, *he* swept through the door.

No one knew his history-
no microchip, no name,
a black and white ball of fluff,
ears larger than his frame.
But he began to meow so loud
that soon he'd drawn an eager crowd.
We set the other forms aside.
"We'll take THAT one!" we quickly cried.

We brought him home, and to begin,
thought Mabel-cat would break him in.
But unlike the teaching we had planned,
'twas the kitten who had clear command.

He wore a tuxedo, wears it still to this day.
He was measured and calm, even in play.
"What shall we call him?", a conundrum for sure.
with his oversized ears, white feet, and black fur.

No Boots, Pounce, or Mittens-
no, no, not for he!
We needed a name with some dignity.

My mother had taught me each cat has three names.
The first one conferred for our daily domains.
The second, per Hamlet's cruel machinations:
"You nickname God's creatures" with dumb
appellations.
These spill out subconscious and we spout willy-nilly
"Dooky whumpus! Pucker Ducker!"
Lord, cats sure make us silly.

The third name is special, a fact of cat pride.
Most humans can't know it, for it's kept deep inside.
But if you love a cat well enough,
he may love you the same,
and whisper one day
his one, true cat name.

For now, our new kitten didn't share his identity
and it was clear from his posture he was *not* a nonentity.
We'd need something with stature- hmmm…well, let's
see…
Then wham! It hit us! Yes, "Henry" he'll be!

His secret name, though, I still haven't guessed.
But while traveling abroad and in Budapest,
I thought of the silly one. Oh, unkindest cut!
It's *Bolyhos Popsi*, which means "fluffy butt."

II
Then comes the thieving filmmaker,
his film school tasks undone,
assigned to make a biopic,
but subjects he had none.

And here dwelled our young hero,
innocent, unspoiled at that.
"I have my subject!" sneered the thief,
"So what if he's a cat?"

Thus spoke Zarathustra:
the Last Man's sloth bodes bad.
if necessity's the mother of invention,
then procrastination is its dad.

So he posed him and deposed him,
caught his steps and mews.
It was certainly not an action pic
since all cats mainly snooze.

But the filmmaker, a creative sort,
found a theme with glee:
a French cat, haughty, worldly, wise
and weighed down with ennui!
The thief took our contented cat,
transformed him to *Henri*.

"We'll make him put upon and bored,
enduring victimhood,
contemptuous of the human horde,
misused, misunderstood."

III

Le Chat Noir debuted online
to moderate acclaim.
But nothing could prepare us all
for Henry's newfound fame
when Henri 2, *Paw de Deux*, ten million viewers strong,
took off like a rocket ship
as we were dragged along.

Much to the family's surprising elation,
our cat had become a viral sensation.

As caretaker to this feline star,
I made one special rule:
he can't be shuffled all about
for a cat, that just seems cruel.

Interviews and featured bits-
they'll have to stop in here.
And thus began a news parade
as they came from far and near.

There was Animal Planet and the <u>LA Times</u>
and <u>People</u> magazine;
the thief filmed Henry at the vet
and loathing Halloween.

A Christmas Dickens parody,
with every household cat,
political snippets, one with a dog,
and one, The Cat Is Sat.

The thieving guy outdid himself,
and soon two books were written.
There was no doubt Henri was loved,
the public awed and smitten.

Some naysayers did appear because
a hater's gotta hate.
"Cat can't speak French!" but the thief replied,
"And his English isn't great…"

Facebook pals soon piled up,
cat people true indeed,
and Henry raised some consciousness
for other cats in need.

I read what fans wrote to my cat,
saw pictures of their crew.
I smiled at most, but if they mourned,
I shed a few tears too.

For we're all connected by such love,
cat people realize,
wherever we live, whatever we speak,
there's universal ties.

III

An internet star? Henry hasn't a clue;
he just acts that way, as all good cats do.
From his puffed out chest to his wrap-around tail,
he sure puts the alpha in our home's alpha male.

As for me, his human servant,
I know all his tricks:
cajoling and bullying for bits of Party Mix.
He plays me like a fiddle, but I just can't say no.
Is he spoiled? A neutral judge
would probably say so.

If other cats challenge him, he turns a bit yellow-
from King of the Hill to mushiest marshmallow.
But he's sweet natured, patient, and does understand
when the thieving filmmaker takes camera in hand.
He'll sit on the table, looking noble and still,
"Ready for my close-up, Mr. DeMille."

We watch our pets age, as all creatures do
while we travel together and grow older too.
Henry and I, retired, content,
a testament to how fast the years went.
And some days I shudder and fear more and more
that sharp arrow of loss aimed deep at my core
when the cat patron, Gertrude, good Saint of Nivelles
porte doucement enfin son âme au Ciel.

But for now, I can sit as he purrs on my lap
and watch on old films my philosopher cat.
Yes, he's been famous, but what counts in the end
is the love he receives from this true human friend.
For all cats are superstars to those they belong-
that's the note to remember from dear Henry's song.

MEET THE CATS OF HENRY'S HOUSEHOLD AND THEIR SILLY NICKNAMES

Henry
Henry Bray-DONE
Henry the Braden
Bolyhos Popsi
Mr. Fluffybutt
Fluffernutter
Fluffabottomus
Taras Bulba Pants
Caca Kitty

Mabel
Nink Poo
Puckerton Buckerton
May-BELLE
Ninky
Mabeletskiy

Ed
Eduardo
Snow Bunny

Ebb
Ebbers
Black Kitty
Ebber-ROOTS
The Ebbster

Gussie
Bed Kitty
Gusalina
Minky Muffin
Alien Cat
Little Girl
Cackette
Grey Kitty
Pudge Pot

Benjamin
Boo
The Big Guy
Boo the Boozer
Boozer the Bruiser

THE IDIOT AND THE ODDITY:
THE EPIC TALE OF HOW ED AND GUSSIE
FOUND THEIR WAY HOME

Prologue
Sit back and hear now our story of kittens, one was
white and one grey.
Like your brother-in-law who won't leave your house,
they stopped not to visit, but stay.
Their mother cat came seeking refuge, but fate threw
the dice in its game,
And the white one though proved to be dumb as a
donut, found shelter and fortune and fame.

❧

Book One
'Twas a rare day in the Emerald City; the sun was
shining so fair,
and when we returned from a bicycle ride, the mom
and her kittens were there.

Some very cruel human had just dumped them off, hungry and sad, but alive.
We surveyed the scene and counted her brood. "Oh no!" we exclaimed, "There are *five!*"

Like the first flowering bud in the spring, a little cat's beauty enthralls,
and the kittens, despite our resolve, still, conquered and tore down our walls.
Bastet, the good goddess of felines, spoke to quiet our hearts all the same,
"I have come to look out for them; these are my small ones. I bid you to let them remain."

Two of the kittens were mixed white and black, and two were pure grey like their mother.
The last was all white and turned out to be the clingiest and the worst bother.

Fed in the yard, the six so amenable, really quite feral, not more.
One day as I sat lacing up my old running shoes, the white one pushed open the door.

Just as a caterpillar climbs up a willow leaf when the trees breathe out their first sap,
the white one came in and sat on my shoe, clawing his way to my lap.

❧

Book Two

Guess then, dear reader, how long was the interval
before the brood came inside.
Confined to one room, well, that didn't work either; all
rules were ignored and defied.

Eight cats in one house soon proved impossible though
Henry and Mabel didn't mind.
We started procedures for feline adoptables, new
homes determined to find.

The goddess Bastet again came to their aid (there must
have been ample cat praying),
though it probably helped that all bills we paid for
neutering, license, and spaying.

❧

Book Three

The white kitty, though, we decided to keep him -
attached to us surely like glue.
And to stave off his loneliness, kept in our household
the grey, fluffy male kitten too.

Ed White we called him, to honor an astronaut, brave
man so noble and true.
And as for the grey one, we named him Gus Grissom.
Our cat house was increased by two.

Surprises though often do come with our felines,
enough to make the head whirl!
The vet on the day of the neutering called us, "You
know that Gus Grissom's a girl?"

So sister to Ed then took the name Gussie and she is
our homebody for sure.
She just hides in the closet or stays on the bed, but
she's sweet, likes to talk, quick to purr.

Thus, we all settled in and we learned over time all the
traits that we see in Ed White:
He's a real momma's boy, a fanatic for laps,
affectionate, not very bright.
He drools when he purrs and cackles at birds, but he
flees loud sounds out of fear.
He jumps on the bed and raises his rump to request a
good whap on his rear.

≈

Book Four
Just as the wolf descends from the mountaintop on the
innocent lamb as it bleats,
just as the carrion crows gnaw the bones of each
carcass laid out on the street,
so the thieving filmmaker seized on poor Ed: "What a
foil for Henri he will be!"
Thus, that fateful morn, L'Imbécile Blanc was born: a
fool for the whole world to see.

≈

Book Five

Some days as I sit and lace up my shoes, Ed drools on
my lap, purrs, and then
his eyes look at mine as if to still say, "can you tell me
the story again-
of the way when I came to you, homeless and scared,
you befriended us, took us all in?"

I answer him, "Sure. Let's praise the cat goddess who
knew just the way it should be.
She helped out your mother, your sisters and brother,
and led you home safely to me."

CAT NICKNAMES SENT TO HENRI'S
FACEBOOK PAGE

Bootsy Princess Pusspants.
Sir Sheds-A-lot the Baron of Underfoot
Jasper, Sir Purzalot
Miss Rose Plushbottom
Fluffybuttamus
Sass-a-mass with a big fluff ass
Miss Velvet Fluffytums
Flubster McTurkey-Thighs
Snowball the Snotrocket
Her Majesty Sabrina, Her Royal Boufiness
Princess Plume Tail
Fatniss Neverclean
Señor Pantaloons Fluffer-wuffer Butt
Buster l'Orange
Fluffernutter Floofydoodle
Sir Nigel Skinnyshanks
Ballozius Whiskarius the First
El Catto Fatto
Poopity Poopmuffin
Madame Saggypants
Rocky, The Reckless and Willful
Violetta Moonflower von Stubbybutt the Funmeister
Princess Poopie-Doop
Professor Charlie Buttons
Macy Couer de Leon Gray aka Meeshie-moo
Fatty McChubster the Kitty Beast
Sneeker Foo Foo
Tigger of Griffindor the Bulbasaur
Señor Sassy Trousers
Gizmo Purrbox
Buddha Belly Boy

Princess Lulu Prissy Pants
Maximus Catimus
Chubkins Bubkins
Spookie-spoo Pussy-poo, the Beast from the East
Stripey-pants the Great
Silliah Sunshine Mischief Wavingtail
Bosco-roni, Full Of Baloney
Twiggy The Piglet
Toby McTabby of the Clan McTabby
Budleus P. Buggins the Third
Oona Flannery Pom-Pom
Princess Buttercream Yum-Yum
Missy Moose Goose
Her Majesty Queen Fluffy Tail
Lord Smellaby Sewer-Butt
Mr. Tricky Paws
Simon Wreck O. Saurus
HunkaChunkaLubs
Miss Sassafras Sassy Pants
SnuggleBunny Bobcat
Señor Faucet Sucker
Babycat Numero Quatro
Guido Hunny-bunny Fortunato
Miss Booty Patootie
Mr. Fuzzbutt-Furryboots
Zephyrniah Catalyst Bum Snuggler
Little Miss Large and in Charge
Mister Poofy Pants
Widdle Miss Sugarpawsie-wawsies
Saffy Bobbles Bon Bon
Bubby Boobers Bubba Pussycat
Jade Empress Daughter of Heaven, Queen of All She
Surveys
Osiris Michael Jackson Quinn

Loki Hammerpants, Goddess of Growl
King Dork of Dorktown
Puddin' Snax
Miss Marrooti-toot-toot
Captain Idiot the Brainless Wonder
Mrs. Tailfeather Bird Butt
Grand Champion Fluffington McPoofBottom

I am surrounded by morons.

TWO SONNETS FOR MABEL

Decision

Mabel-Cat! This, our eighteenth September
and now come to our last one.
But we can sit here in the sun,
and I'll close my eyes and still remember
my memories of you so fresh and tender,
your feistiness when young.
But look what you've become:
so tired and ready to surrender.

The thought of your passing, I cannot abide
but old-age maladies wore you out.
We once fended them off, there's no doubt.
But now, my six-toed calico,
I must lower the drawbridge and allow them inside.
It's long past time to let you go.

Passage

The kindly vet has come out our way
to ease your passing, dearest one.
Oh, Mabel, haven't we had a good run?
We named you for the month of May
when we brought you home on that first day.
Now, last tail twitch of irritation;
then she checks your pulse and says, "It's done."
But I'll hold you a moment more and stay.

There's a stillness this twilight, a hushed tendency.
The earth has gone quiet, barely a sound.
Crows fly over, all eastward bound.
Distant notes of a robin song.
My old one, Nink Poo, now your light shines in me,
so rest soft. You're here, just where you belong.

THE BLACK CAT WHO IS MY NEIGHBORS'

My four cats know that he's an interloper
and he senses he's here on approval.
More shy than the rest,
he knows he's a guest,
and lives in fear of imminent removal.

He slipped in uninvited through the cat door one day,
and it was clear to all which place he favors.
He purrs upon my lap,
sleeps nearby when I nap,
but he really isn't mine- he is the neighbors'.

Yet who can read the workings of the feline mind?
And what cat in fact belongs to any owner?
He delivers to the house
the occasional dead mouse
to compensate for being just a loaner.

The other cats belt him if he enters their circumference,
so snobby and secure in sovereignty!
To them I am just staff,
but I save him from their wrath,
and for that, he does seem truly fond of me.

So, here's to my one ally in the battle for control.
They drive him out, but he demonstrates persistence.
Against this Fascist clowder,
it couldn't make me prouder
that the black cat's with the Socialist Resistance.

It's now been several years since the black cat just
moved in
And mostly, we have a peaceful crew.
The neighbors gave no flack,
didn't really want him back,
with his old life, this cat's definitely through.

Fastidious he ain't: he's a raggedy guy for sure.
He doesn't wash like all the other cats.
Constant dander dooms him
and though the family grooms him,
his fur stays perpetually in mats.

He's always there to eat, though he is the Vomit King.
His ears pick up the sound of any can.
But the cat food he's ingested
is ejected undigested.
I could dump it on the floor and skip the middleman.

He's got irritating ways to be always underfoot.
He somehow filled his cat mind with the notion
that our kindness is a scam,
so he must be on the lam,
and run away in furtive locomotion.

His ears are notched and scarred, showing signs of past
tough fights.
But in the house, he usually is cool.
When he's had enough of Ed,
he beats him up instead.
The black cat does not tolerate a fool.

So here is some advice about felines we take in:
be kind and sure, put out the welcome mat.
But for many that you meet,
you can get them off the street,
but you won't get the street
out of the cat.

BENJAMIN

For many a day, he would not come to me,
but crouched at the top outside stair,
refused to approach; he wouldn't dare.
He watched and his gaze cut right though me.

For his eyes had a feral cat's stare.
He seemed indeed like no pet.
He'd a tiger's tail stripe and a panther's rosette,
his ears tipped with ebony hair.

The outstretched paws were as huge as they get,
like a snow leopard perched on his peak.
I tried to approach him and speak,
thinking it's time that we met.

He lived in the house just over the street.
Benjamin the name, but his mom called him Boo,
said he was crazy and part Bengal too,
explaining that marbled coat and huge feet.

He ventured here often all summer through,
but I never would say we were friends or attached.
If I tried to pet him, I was bitten and scratched.
The other cats thought his forays would not do.

But his sleuthing skills were strong and unmatched.
Once he found the cat door, we had no relief.
His talent was great as freeloader and thief-
leftover kibble was found fast and snatched.

He was sure a beauty but gave me such grief,
and due to his size, my cats found him scary.
I looked into his eyes and asked, "Why are you wary?
Do you think I would harm you? Why this belief?"

❧

Benjamin's Answer: What A Cat Is

-I am the cat, that
stands on my own.
My jeweled eyes spy
the quickest of prey.
They do not escape: I soon have them at bay.
You cannot follow, for I hunt alone.

I seek out the weak ones who stay
shaking in burrows so deep.
Keep hiding! I think. They don't make a peep,
but my ears hear their breath anyway.

There's many a field mouse to reap.
I lurk in the autumn moonlight.
I'll hunt them again the next night.
Now, content and sated, I sleep.

You see, all cats, we have our own code.
Catch us and try as you might,
we know that you have no true right
to think nature's an object you're owed.

You bound the proud horse as a captive you rode,
took sheep, cows, and pigs for their wool and meat,
turned wild grasslands into your wheat,
and made the poor donkey carry your load.

Many a canine I've seen cruel men beat
if they failed to perform just as you bid.
The wolf has become a sad balm for your id,
made to heel as a servant next to your feet.

But I stood apart and saw what you did.
I am the cat, the one who didn't bend.
I never wanted you for a friend.
Man is the creature I chose to forbid.

-But Benj, didn't we partner on rats and do fine?

-Partner with *you*? Oh, no, not a bit.
Don't flatter yourselves- I cared not a whit.
The choice to dwell in your houses was mine.

We peeked through the door and I must admit:
inside, we found so much to admire:
a platter of milk and a seat by your fire.

-Aha, true then! That invite was man's to permit.

-Foolish human, you're such a bad liar!
It was we who picked comfort, lives filled with ease,
But we can go back to the wild when we please.
Yet you - soft, diminished - you're now a creation
of this prison you've made called *civilization*.

Yes, we cats are *with* you, but not *of* you, you see.
We're a small, remnant thread to what you used to be.
You sense it still, and it hurts you within
when the blue moon is full and you feel the north wind.
For a little insurance, you just traded it in.

You traded it in and now bear the cost.
I'm the constant reminder of what you have lost,
for I stand apart and keep secret my name.
At the last, it was only yourselves you made tame.

৵

Epilogue

I was quiet when he finished, because in the end,
a cat's a cat for all that, and won't bend;
it is us sorry humans I cannot comprehend.

Yet, who knows with time what may occur?
Benj began to allow me to touch his sleek fur.
But he often didn't trust me- that was clearly a fact:
he'd flick fast his tail and I'd get my hand whacked.
Till one morning, surprising, but I felt it for sure-
that throaty vibration of a definite purr.

Now, Benj visits daily and we somewhat agree
on the story of felines that he's tried to teach me.
What I should call him, I just somehow knew:
his secret, third name, the one that was true.
For he is the Cat, who stands proud and apart,
the living reflection of my own lost Wild Heart.

ABOUT THE AUTHOR

Kathleen Braden is privileged to have been not only the caretaker for Henri le Chat Noir, but also for a clowder of other cats who seem to have a knack for just showing up. She is a retired Professor of Geography at Seattle Pacific University and assists her son, Will Braden, with CatVideoFest SPC to raise funds for animal shelters around the globe.

Made in the USA
Columbia, SC
12 January 2021